A Journey to Greatness

Living a Life of Excellence

By Darron Gillion

Breezeway Books

ISBN: 978-1-62550-577-4 (PB)
        978-1-62550-578-1 (EB)

Library of Congress Control Number: 2011900816

Definitions

Ex.cuses (Ik-skyoos-es)
- A reason to do something one may want to do or avoid something one may not want to do.

La.zi.ness (lay-zee-nes)
- To avoid work or exertion : no energy or vigor.

Pro.cras.ti.na.tion (pro-krasti-naysh'n)
- To postpone or delay doing something; To put off for a later time.

Quit.ting (kwit-ting)
- To give up without a fight.

Dis.trac.tions (di-skra-shun)
- To draw focus away from something or someone.

Ig.nor.ance (ig-nor-ans)
- Unaware of information; lack of knowledge.

Ha.tred (hate-red)
- To be consumed with hate

In.sults (in-sults)
- To belittle or affront; to offend.

Im.pa.tient (im-pa-shunt)
- Unwilling to wait.

Dis.hon.es.ty (dis-un-uh-stee)
- To lie; to cheat
- To operate in fraud

Rude.ness (rood-nes)
- Unmannerly
- Rough
- Without courtesy

UN.for.give.ness (uhn-fer-giv-nes)
- Unwilling to forgive
- To show no mercy

Me.di.oc.ri.ty (mee-dee-ok-ri-tee)
- State of being ordinary; settling with average.
- Neither bad nor good.

Dis.re.spect (dis-re-spekt)
- To disregard
- To treat rudely

Pho.ni.ness (fon-ni-nes)
- Not real; fake.
- Not genuine.

Ar.ro.gance (ar-uh-guhns)
- Without humility
- To think more of ones self than they ought

In.con.sist.en.cy (in-kun-sis-tun-see)
- Unsteady; unreliable
- Out of harmony

Non.cha.lant (non-shu-luhnt)
- Without care
- Unexcited

Neg.a.tiv.i.ty (neg-uh-tiv-uh-tee)
- An atmosphere with negative thoughts, attitudes or speech.
- Without or low expectations.

Introduction

*T*his book was conceived after I talked to a co-worker about the behavior of a friend's son. I tried to convey to my two sons that they should never settle for average but should try to achieve greatness in every arena and every aspect of their lives.

When I was in junior high, life was all about getting "in" with the popular crowd and making sure one was wearing "in style" clothes. My history teacher would often say, "Greatness is not just automatic; it has to be developed." We would all laugh because

1

of the way he would throw his finger in the air and speak with so much sincerity; it struck us as funny. Besides, we thought, life was easy; all we had to do was make it past lunch, and the rest of the day went by very quickly, or so we thought.

Now I understand what that old history teacher was trying to tell us. Greatness does not come automatically; it has to be developed, nourished, and cultivated; it has to be fed integrity, character, knowledge, and determination.

In this book I give a few metaphors to illuminate a clear path to achieving greatness. This book is not a one-time read; you can always refer to it. Each and every person has a purpose and a degree of greatness to achieve, and he or she can use this book as a tool to reach goals. Your DNA is encrypted with everything you're destined to be. You can be a better father, mother, husband, wife, student, or just a better person, but you will need knowledge, determination, and guidance to help you achieve your goals.

Excellence Is a Magnet
That Attracts Greatness

Greatness is not something you take from the outside and put inside; it's something that's already inside of you that needs to come out. I won't say that greatness never comes easily; situations sometimes push us to greatness all by themselves. When you put on the garment of excellence, it propels you to great achievement.

You have to make a decision to succeed, because if you wait for someone or the perfect moment to arrive, your chances of success will be few and far between. Greatness starts with a decision. Greatness shouldn't be something we gamble with. It's like throwing our efforts into the darkness and hoping that they land on something that will push us to greatness. Greatness is perfected by the tools of patience, hard work, and knowledge.

Some may ask, "What's the big deal about greatness?" The truth is that great men and women can change the course of a nation, whether they propose an idea, make a new discovery, or perform a heroic deed. They can change the momentum of a business, a church, a school, or a community.

Excellence is a magnet that attracts greatness; it is the ability to master a task and perform it with few if any errors every time.

To master an endeavor, talent, or skill is to perform it with little or no thought. For example, when you first learn to ride a bike, you concentrate on balance and pedaling. After you have mastered bike riding, you don't think about falling. One of the ways to master something is to practice it over and over again until you can perform it effortlessly.

Excuses

Ex.cuses (ik-skyoozes)
- *Reasons given for doing something or not doing something.*

Excuses are the killers of success; they hunt down great potential and subdue it. They seek out ambition and silence it. Excuses provide a back door to escape greatness.

The excuses we're talking about are the excuses we use to get out of doing something we don't want to do. Have you ever noticed that whenever a situation comes up, we use that situation as an excuse not to do something we don't want to do, but if it's something that we want to do, our situation becomes an obstacle that needs to be overcome?

For example, let's say a friend invites you to a conference on how to help others to overcome fear. The conference is thirty miles away, and you really don't want to go, but you don't want to disappoint your friend. All of a sudden you get a phone call from another friend who needs you to pick him up from an airport that's thirty miles in the opposite direction. Now the situation calls for your going thirty miles in the opposite direction, and you use this as an excuse not to attend the conference.

On the other hand, using the same scenario, let's say a friend invites you to a concert that you've being waiting to attend. But then you get a call from another friend, same as before, who needs you to pick him up from the airport thirty miles in the opposite direction. In this case the thirty miles is an obstacle rather than an excuse.

On the other hand:

Non-excuses are the breath of success; they give success life. They encourage responsibility and leadership. Non-excuses are part of a coalition that brings forth greatness, and those who employ non-excuses consistently will always be on the cutting edge.

Laziness

La.zi.ness (lay-zee-nes)
- *The avoidance of work or exertion; demonstrating no energy or vigor.*

*L*aziness is a seed of failure that produces the fruit of missed opportunities, leaving one destitute and empty. Those who eat of it find themselves malnourished even in the abundance of life.

Laziness is not something someone is born with; it's a bad habit that was formed. I was told it takes twenty-one days to form a habit and twenty-one days to break it. So if laziness is a habit that you have developed, you will have to come up with a plan to break it. You might have to find things to keep you busy throughout the day. Some of us are just lazy when it comes to certain things. For example, we may work hard at our job, but when it comes to working around the house, we become lazy and get nothing done. So you will have to come up with a plan to address laziness.

On the other hand:

Hard work is a strong tree whose roots are anchored deep, whose branches reach far and wide to places one never thought could be reached. Those who eat of its sweet fruit can always see wealth and success within reach. Hard work brings the satisfaction of knowing that you gave it your all, which will yield results.

Procrastination

Pro.cras.ti.na.tion (pro-krasti-naysh'n)
- *Postponing or delaying doing something; putting something off to a later time.*

*P*rocrastination is a self-inflicted wound that festers and attracts disappointment, humiliation, and mediocrity; it's a virus that germinates and results in little or no success.

Procrastination is another bad habit; it's something you have to work against on purpose. I have seen many great opportunities missed because of procrastination.

One way to fight against procrastination is "to just get up and do it."

There are many reasons why people procrastinate; one reason is because of comfort zones. When we're comfortable, we prefer not to move or change, but when we are uncomfortable, we try to change things. For example, if the due date for taxes is April 15 and it's just February, everything is alright, because you have another two months to go, and taxes can wait. But if you wait until April 14, getting your taxes done is at the top of your priority list. We will force ourselves to get our taxes done to avoid the discomfort of being penalized by the IRS.

On the other hand:

Just getting something done is a reliable method of hitting the mark perfectly every time. It removes the rain cloud of burden from over your head. It eliminates the potential of laziness; it brings the comfort of knowing that something is complete. To get things done captures opportunities to get ahead.

Quitting

Quit.ting (kwit-ting)
- *Giving up without a fight.*

Quitting is the pathway to no-where, and those who walk this pathway are led into a vicious cycle that goes round and round, yielding no positive results in life. Quitting will always cause you to look back with regret.

Quitting is tricky; you have to know when to quit and when not to quit. My father told me a story. "In a small town there was a fair that offered hot air balloon rides. Somehow the balloon came loose, and all the men of the town rushed over and grabbed the rope, trying to hold the balloon down. One man shouted, 'Hold on, men.' They held with all their might but could not hold the balloon down. It began to get away. Someone shouted out, 'Let go, men.' All the men let go except one. The balloon ascended higher and higher with the one man still holding on. The people on the ground yelled, 'Let go! Let go!' until the balloon got too high; that's when they changed their yells to, 'Hang on! Hang on!'

The time to quit is when something is destroying us. We should hang on to the things that are making us stronger, even though they are not always easy to do. People often admire others who have a nicely shaped body, but the workouts necessary to achieve that nicely shaped body are not easy.

On the other hand:

Persistence is the weapon that pierces through defeat and failure. It does not take no for an answer; it refuses to stay down. It will go against the odds and see victory. Persistence is the lifesaver that pulls you in when you have fallen overboard and are afloat in the massive sea of life.

Distraction

Dis.trac.tion (di-skra-shun)

- *An element that draws focus away from something or someone.*

Distraction is an enemy to our arriving at our destiny: great achievement. Those who are lured away by it are left alone and unsatisfied with life. Distractions are false impressions of contentment that rob us of life's most precious and valuable commodity, which is time.

Distractions are not always bad, but they can result in bad timing, they can take us away from the task at hand, and they can cause us to lose focus.

In almost every action movie there's a rescue scene in which a comrade has been captured and a hero says, "We need a distraction." Distractions will cause a responsible person to behave irresponsibly; they will cause a productive person to become unproductive. Some distractions can become an addiction.

On the other hand:
Focusing is an intense beam of light that burns through walls of opposition, making a pathway through all kinds of uncertainties. Those who shine this light will eliminate the darkness of confusion and stand tall and strong, like powerful lighthouses that shine through great storms and guide others to safe and dry grounds.

Ignorance

Ig.nor.ance (ig-nor-ans)
- *The state of being unaware of information or knowledge.*

*I*gnorance is not progress standing still; it's falling backward. Lack of knowledge is not a get-out-of-jail-free card; it's an imprisonment of dreams. Those who allow it to live within them will always face closed doors in life.

I disagree with the old phrase, "What you don't know can't hurt you." What you don't know can destroy you. If science knew the cure for cancer, many lives would be saved.

I talked with one of my sons about all the great men in history who had achieved great things. I told him that all men are created equal and that no one had any super powers that gave them the ability to do things that they couldn't otherwise do. I told my son that the only difference between him and other great men is that they knew something that he did not know...yet. One of the greatest but easiest ways to gain knowledge is reading. Many great achievers have put all they know in books, and anyone can gain the knowledge they had by simply reading their books.

On the other hand:

Knowledge is a key that unlocks the doors of opportunity, success, and promotion. Those who use this key will find themselves entering new rooms of adventure, new possibilities, and fulfillment in life.

Hatred

Ha.tred (hate-red)
- *The feeling of intense aversion.*

*H*atred is a poison that spoils life and everything connected to it. It rots the pillars of joy, peace, and love, which are the strengths of every person. Those who exercise hatred will find themselves on a downward spiral.

Hatred is a parasite; the more you feed it, the more it grows. It divides and conquers the one who hates. To not hate does not mean having a warm fuzzy feeling about everyone you meet or trusting everyone. There are always some people with whom you will have personality clashes— you won't like the way they talk or eat or something else about them—but this does not mean that you have to hate that person. If I choose to hate someone, it will harm me more than the one I hate; it will detract from me. Is it easy not to hate? I must confess that there are some people who make it so easy for others to hate them, but if we find ourselves in this position, we need to say to ourselves, "I choose not to hate."

On the other hand:

Love is the antivenom that fights the poison of hate. It brings wholeness and wellness to individuals as well as to relationships. Love is the antibiotic that brings healing to your soul.

Those who inject themselves with love will experience a healthier life of joy and peace.

Insult

In.sult (in-sult)
- *A belittlement or affront; an offense.*

*I*nsults are knives that slice away the character and esteem of others, and those who master their use will never be considered trustworthy. Insults are mirrors that reflect the heart of the one who uses them. They are a wall that hides one's own flaws and insecurities.

It takes no special skills to insult someone, and cutting someone else down will never build you up. Making someone look small will never make

33

you look big. Pointing out someone's flaws will never hide your own. Making someone feel bad about him or herself will never make you feel good about yourself. Sometimes it's best to try to keep your insults to yourself. It's not easy, but if you practice doing it, you will find that insulting others is not really necessary.

King Solomon, considered one of the wisest kings of Israel, said, "A fool is considered wise until he opens his mouth."

One of my elementary teachers would tell me all the time, "Darron, God gave you two ears and one mouth so you can listen twice as much as you talk." Sometimes our mouth gets us into situations we wished we had never gotten into.

On the other hand:

Compliments are the needle and thread that sew together security and confidence. They are powerful elements that fight against low self-esteem. Compliments are mirrors that reflect the heart of those who use them. Compliments reveal the security felt by the one who gives them freely.

Impatience

Im.pa.tience (im-pa-shuns)
- *Unwillingness to wait.*

*I*mpatience is a loose step on the stairway of life. One misstep, and dreams, plans, and visions can stumble and fall back to ground level. Those who choose to be impatient put their lives on fast forward and miss the gifts and precious moments that life can bring.

Patience is a quality that most people don't have but everybody needs. It's also a quality that is not being promoted these days. "Quicker" and "faster" seem to be selling much better. Impatience is prevalent in all of us; I find myself screaming at red lights if I miss the green light.

Patience is a stepping stone to consistency, and consistency is a stepping stone to good results. Good results are increased and forward motion. Sometimes impatience will cause our mouth to take off before it gets its marching orders from our brain, and that can make us end up with our foot in our mouth. Remember what King Solomon said: "Even a fool is considered wise until he opens his mouth."

On the other hand:

Patience is the concrete that builds a well-rounded character; it allows you to hear the whole story and see the complete picture. Those who build with this concrete will find themselves standing before a skyscraper of good and well-thought-out decisions.

Patience is the leash that holds back untamed tongues.

Dishonesty

Dis.hon.es.ty (dis-un-uh-stee)
- *Lying; cheating.*
- *Fraudulent behavior.*

*D*ishonesty is a sandy foundation for any relationship; it causes corrosion from the inside. It eats away at trust, teamwork, and camaraderie. Those who build upon it will soon experience disaster.

Honesty seems to be so inconvenient, while dishonesty seems to be one of life's shortcuts. It may seem as though you get further, and have an easier road by being dishonest.

But being dishonest is like trying to reach high while standing on a broken ladder balanced on a board that is on a rubber ball: everything will soon come crashing down. Honesty may be inconvenient at times, but it ultimately works out as the best policy. I remind my sons, "If you do what's right, right will come to you." Truth will always rise to the surface no matter how deep you bury it.

On the other hand:

Honesty is the solid foundation of life that will stand against the earthquake of distrust. Honesty points out all the need-to-know details that eliminate unnecessary pain and hard work. Those who stand on this foundation will find themselves on solid ground and in good company.

Rudeness

Rude.ness (rood-nes)
- *Unmannerly bearing.*
- *Roughness.*
- *Lack of common courtesy.*

Rudeness is a stench that fills the atmosphere and repels key connections in life. It's a mask that hides true beauty. It cancels the opportunity for great friendships.

A rude person is disliked even by family and friends. A rude person is like a runaway train or a wild animal that might attack anybody, so people simply stay away. People love to see the tables turned on those who are rude, who usually find themselves empty and alone.

On the other hand:

Kindness is a flower that draws others with its sweet, pleasant fragrance and beautiful, bright colors. Kindness is the handle that gives you access to new and exciting friendships.

Unforgivingness

Un.for.giv.ing.ness (uhn-fer-giv-ing-niss)
- *Unwillingness to forgive.*

*B*eing unforgiving means incurring a debt that can never be paid; interest on this debt accrues at a rate double the day before. Those who buy in on it will find themselves emotionally and spiritually bankrupt and in a place they never wanted to go.

Being unforgiving is like shooting yourself in the foot and expecting someone else to yell out in pain. The lack of forgiveness is a misfiring gun; even though you aim it at someone else it always fire backwards. There is one common misconception about forgiveness: many think that just because you forgive an individual you can also trust him or her; this is far from the truth. Trust is not free; it has to be worked for.

Mediocrity

Me.di.oc.ri.ty (mee-dee-ok-ri-tee)
- *The state of being ordinary; settling for average.*
- *Being neither bad nor good.*

*M*ediocrity is a valley so deep that the sunshine of greatness and success never shines there. It's a muddy road of life that causes one to become stuck, never moving forward or backward.

Mediocrity is a mindset that will hold great men and women down. Mediocrity is almost worse than going backwards, because those going backwards know at least where they are going. Mediocrity is hanging out in limbo and being comfortable there. The mindset of those who choose to be mediocre is, "If I do more, people will expect more out of me all the time." One must decide on greatness and excellence and pursue those goals.

On the other hand:

Excellence is the road map that helps an individual navigate the journey of life. It's the solid foundation for every terrain one may encounter. It refuses to remain stationary even after achieving a high plateau.

Disrespect

Dis.re.spect (dis-re-spekt)
- *A sense of disregard.*
- *Dismissive rudeness.*

Disrespect is a tree planted on rocky soil; it has weak roots and yields poor fruit. Those who cultivate this tree will find themselves discarded and isolated.

Disrespect is a tricky one; there may be individuals whom you feel do not deserve respect because respect is earned. The aged and those in authority should be respected. If you feel that an individual in authority does not deserve respect, you still have to respect that person's position.

On the other hand:

Respect is the root that produces fruit that attracts others. Respect anchors itself in good soil and produces good fruit. Respect attracts respect; if you show respect to someone, most of the time he or she will give it right back. And, very important, you have to respect yourself before others can truly respect you.

Phoniness

Pho.ni.ness (fo-ni-nes)
- *Being not real; fake.*
- *The quality of being not genuine.*

P honiness is a blanket that covers and hides the real person. It's a fragile shell that crumbles to the touch, leaving one empty and scared. Those who seek cover under it will ultimately lose themselves.

Phoniness is trying to be something you're not. It's a wall that you hide behind because of the fear that others will not accept the real you. It's hard to connect with a person who is being phony. Have you ever tried to connect with a person but for some reason you just couldn't? It may be because that person has not revealed his or her true self, and you were trying to connect with a person who was revealing just an outer shell.

On the other hand:

Realness is the source of courage that shows no fear of revealing itself. Realness believes that others are more than just games who need to be "played." Realness is not hypocritical in any way.

Arrogance

Ar.ro.gance (ar-uh-gins)
- *The lack of humility.*
- *The tendency to think more of one's self than one should.*

*A*rrogance is a tool of false confidence, and the work it produces is fear of rejection; those who use it will never experience true personal growth.

Arrogance is a sign of low self-esteem. Arrogant people may feel that if they don't pat themselves on the back, no one will. They may feel that if they don't reaffirm themselves, who will? Arrogant people have a great fear of rejection and abandonment. Humility is not being weak; it's being strong and under control.

On the other hand:

Humility is an exploding power of confidence and self-esteem. Those who ignite this power will find themselves rising above criticism, negativity, and traps of others. Those who are humble will never have to exclaim their greatness. Humility will speak out for them without words.

Inconsistency

In.con.sis.ten.cy (in-kun-sis-tun-see)
- *Unsteadiness; unreliability.*
- *Lack of harmony.*

*I*nconsistency is a force in motion that gets nowhere. It promises skills that are not mastered, and those who are inconsistent will do a lot but get nothing done.

Inconsistency is the lack of discipline and organization in life. Consistency contains great power. At a McDonald's one day, I pointed out to my two sons a groove in the concrete under a water spout. I told them that rainwater had formed that groove. When they asked me how, I responded, "By a consistent flow." Inconsistency, on the other hand, results in the inability to master anything.

On the other hand:

Consistency is the mighty river that sweeps everything up stream. Consistency moves things that others will tell you can't be moved; it changes things that others will insist can never be changed; it reaches things that others say are unreachable.

Nonchalance

Non.cha.lance (non-shu-lahns)
- *The state of being without care.*
- *Disinterestedness; apathy.*

Nonchalance is the icy cold water that extinguishes the fiery drive to move ahead and be the best. It weakens your ability to prepare, to get the maximum results.

It is easier to deal with someone who refuses to do something upfront than it is to deal with someone who says they will do something but do so only half-heartedly. You can burn plenty of energy trying to motivate and encourage someone who really doesn't want to do something. It's hard to trust a nonchalant person to perform a task in a timely manner and with excellence.

On the other hand:

Passion is the flame that starts the fire of determination, which in turn burns and fuels the desire to achieve above average.

Negativity

Neg.a.tiv.i.ty (neg-uh-tiv-uh-tee)
- *A state of being characterized by negative thoughts, attitudes, or speech.*
- *With low or no expectations.*

Negativity is the weight that plunges you into the deep dark depths of the sea of life. Negativity has no handles to pull one up from the pits of life. Those who connect to negativity will find themselves robbed of hope and serenity.

Being positive does not mean ignoring or neglecting problems or situations; it just means finding a way around or through them. A negative or a positive attitude will induce an atmosphere that is conducive to that emotion for its own survival. A negative attitude will produce a negative atmosphere, where the negative attitude will simply thrive.

On the other hand:

Being positive means having a free-flowing spirit that rises above life's pitfalls; it produces hope and inspiration. Those who grab hold of it will find themselves rising to new heights.

Low Self-Esteem

Low.self.e.steem (loh-self-i-steem)
- *The state of thinking and believing one is less than what they really are.*

*L*ow self-esteem is a vacuum that sucks away our ambition to reach our destiny. Our destiny is what defines our purpose. Low self-esteem obscures our ability to envision achievement and success.

Low self-esteem comes from listening to lies others may have told us or lies we may have told ourselves. People will say things to you that can spark a downward spiral: "You'll never amount to anything. You'll never change. You'll never achieve anything great." No one knows what tomorrow will bring. Shoot for greatness in spite of what others may say or think.

We must be careful with low self-esteem and high self-esteem, we must remain balanced. Some put their weakness in the forefront and hide their strengths behind them. Others put their strengths in the forefront and hide their weakness behind. Our strengths should be celebrated and our weaknesses worked on, not ignored.

On the other hand:

Self-esteem is the push that launches us forward in spite of roadblocks, setbacks, or hang-ups. It

always tells us that we can go further,
we can do more, and we can be more.

Passivity

Pas.siv.ity (pas-sif-fity)
- *Lack of enthusiasm.*

*B*eing passive is a thin, brittle rope that snaps from the tension inherent in trying to pull in a sense of peace and maintaining a low profile. It simply attracts frustration and aggravation. Those who use this rope will find themselves always behind, trying to catch up, and being misused.

Being passive is waiting to see what will happen. You find yourself being reactive instead of being proactive.

You can prevent fires rather than trying to extinguish small fires here and there after they have already started. Being passive is standing still and allowing things to run over you.

On the other hand:

Being proactive will cause things to run more smoothly. Being proactive is a thick, strong line that when cast pulls in prosperity, peace of mind, and leadership. Those who use this line will find themselves ahead of the game.

Rebelliousness

Re.bel.li.ous.ness (ree-bel-y-us-niss)
- *A rising up against authority.*

Rebelliousness is a clog that stops the flow of inner beauty, good ambitions, and a good life. Rebellion is an earplug that closes out truth. Those who practice rebellion will reap only failure and lose in the process.

Rebellion will make you think you're right and everyone else is wrong; it will have you thinking that everyone is against you. It will make you think that it's you against the world, daring anyone to challenge you. Rebellion is contagious; if you listen to the arguments or grievances of a rebellious person, you might be drawn in.

On the other hand:

Cooperation is a lubricant that allows things to run more smoothly and encourages others to place confidence in you. Being cooperative will allow you to be considered reliable, understanding, and a "team" player.

Greed

Greed (greed)
- *A raging desire for wealth or possessions.*

Greed is a mirage of peace, happiness, and satisfaction. Greed will have you diving into the sands of depression, sadness, and unquenchable thirst; the more you get, the more you want. Those who fail to recognize this mirage will find themselves sitting in the desert of life, emotionally and spiritually dehydrated.

Greed can cause the downfall of a nation, community, family, or individual. It is blind to compassion

69

or the needs of others. Those who are greedy always have a lingering fear of the well running dry, while those who are generous are more concerned about the needs of others.

On the other hand:

Generosity is a seed that's planted and yields fruit. It is the push that propels one to become the champion of others. It's a source of joy that brings satisfaction and completion. The key to your success is to find someone else to bless.

Insecurity

In.se.cur.i.ty (in-sir-kur-i-tee)
- *Self-doubt; lack of confidence.*

*I*nsecurity is a sharp, jagged edge that will hurt the ones who are the closest. It slices through trust, love, and honesty. Insecurity will embed itself within a relationship and eat at it from the inside.

Insecurity is not just a lack of trust in others; it's also a lack of trust in one's self. You don't trust that you're good enough or pretty enough. Insecure people wait for others to determine their worth. The only way to overcome insecurity is by believing in yourself. You don't need someone else to determine who you are. The best is inside of you; allow it to come out. Being secure means never having to give in to peer pressure.

On the other hand:

Security is the shield that blocks the arrows of insults, distrust, and low self-esteem. It shields you from the constant fire of negativity. Security is the voice that constantly tells you who you are.

Standoffishness

Stand.off.ish.ness (Stand-aw-fish-niss)
- *Unapproachability; personal coldness or unfriendliness.*

Standoffishness is the smoke that chokes friendship and fellowship and clouds the pathway to companionship. Those who dwell within this smoke will eventually be overcome with loneliness. This smoke will strangle their dreams and achievements.

Having friends is a joy. Knowing that someone cares for you even if he or she is not around is the basis of friendship. Those who choose not to gain friends choose thereby to limit their accomplishments. Standing alone in this world can be very difficult at times, while finding a good friend is like finding a treasure of gold, diamonds, and precious stones.

On the other hand:

Friendship is the fresh air that blows in happiness, companionship, and resources. It also blows life into a wider community. Those who bask in the sunshine of friendship find themselves inhaling great joy and a sense of life.

Doubtfulness

Doubt.ful.ness (Dout-full-ness)
  - *Lack of belief; being in a realm of unbelief.*

*D*oubtfulness is an announcer that proclaims defeat before the game even begins. Doubtfulness shouts out, "You'll never make it! It will never work! Things just won't work out."

To become doubtful is to exercise doubting, to constantly focus on the possibility of failing.

On the other hand:
  Faith is the work that produces action that reveals what one really believes. For example, if I have faith

that it will rain, I'll grab an umbrella before I leave my home. Faith leads one to be optimistic. Faith will strengthen those who are weak and encourage those who are discouraged.

Author's Notes

It's my prayer that this book has enlightened and encouraged you to take the right path toward greatness and that you have decided to become a person of excellence.

My thanks go to Sam Ellis for his insights, on which this book is based.

My thanks go also to my sons, Darron Gillion, Jr. (DJ), a man of wisdom, and Reuben Gillion, a man of ambition. You guys keep me focused on what's really important.

I also thank my mother, Deloris, and father, Albert Sr., for always encouraging me to be a better person in all areas of my life.

Thanks go to my mother-in-law, Rebecca Kirksey, for always encouraging me and seeing so much in me.

Special thanks are reserved for my queen, Rebecca Gillion, for believing in me and making my dreams and visions her own. She is a woman of greatness with a great deal inside her.

Thanks go finally to God, who has given me a gift and allowed me to share it with others.

www.ingramcontent.com/pod-product-compliance
Lightning Source LLC
Chambersburg PA
CBHW062022040426
42447CB00010B/2100